13 Simple Client Follow-Up Strategies

By Mj Callaway, CSP, CVP

13 Simple Client Follow-Up Strategies:

Skip Useless "Checking In" Messages and Get More Sales

By Mj Callaway, CSP, CVP

13 Simple Client Follow-Up Strategies: Skip Useless "Checking In" Messages and Get More Sales

Copyright © 2022 Mj Callaway

All Rights Reserved

Published by: Mj Callaway Training & Development

No part of this publication may be reproduced, stored in or introduced into a retrieval system, or transmitted, in any form, or by any means (electronic, mechanical, photocopying, recording, or otherwise), except as permitted under Section 107 or 108 of the 1976 United States Copyright Act, without written permission of the author. Permission requests should be directed to Mj@MjCallaway.com or P.O. Box 94, Presto, PA 15142 and should be addressed Requests for Permission.

Limit of Liability/Disclaimer. While the author has used best efforts in preparing this book, they make no representations or warranties with respect to the accuracy or completeness of the contents of this book and specifically disclaim any implied warranties of merchantability or fitness for a particular purpose. No warranty may be created or extended. The advice and strategies contained herein may not be suitable for your situation. You should consult with a professional where appropriate. The author shall not be liable for damages arising from the book.

Library of Congress Cataloging-in-Publication Data:

Callaway, Mj

13 Simple Client Follow-Up Strategies: Skip Useless "Checking In" Messages and Get More Sales/Mj Callaway

    Includes bibliographical references

    Includes index

    ISBN: 978-1-7342649-0-6

Printed in the United States of America

Dedication

To everyone who has had to write a follow-up message,

this book is for you. Here's to helping more people and getting more clients!

Table of Contents

Foreword by Gail Gloeckl 1

   The Why Behind This Book 2

Strategy 1: Jog Their Memory With Three Bullets .. 5

Strategy 2: It's Party Time With A
Milestone Celebration 9

Strategy 3: Get Innovative With National Days 13

Strategy 4: Do What Influencers Do 17

Strategy 5: I Want What She's Having 21

Strategy 6: Invite To A Special Event 23

Strategy 7: Questions Are The
 Key To Unlocking Secrets 27

Strategy 8: Are You Making Life Easier For Buyers?
 31

Strategy 9: Do You Have Ways To
Save Buyers Time Or Money? 35

Strategy 10: Share A Valuable Article 39

Strategy 11: Highlight A Startling Statistic 43

Strategy 12: Promote An Icon Idea 47

Strategy 13: Be Our Podcast Guest 51

Foreword
Gail Gloeckl

Mj Callaway makes client communication an art form, as demonstrated in her new mini-book *13 Simple Client Follow-Up Strategies*. She shows us how to turn mundane emails into thought-provoking correspondence. This gem of a book provides me with numerous uh-huh moments that have lightbulbs popping up in my mind on every page. In a world of endless voice mail, text messages, and excess marketing emails, Mj demonstrates how to make follow-up emails concise but exciting. Her strategies will entice clients to respond. My recommendation is that this book should be on the desk of all employees who deal with prospects and customers

The Why Behind This Book

During a presentation for an association, one participant asked, *"How do you follow-up with prospects without saying I'm checking in, or I'm following up?"*

In a conversation with the president of a multi-million dollar commercial heating and air conditioning company, he shared, *"My technicians never follow-up after giving an estimate. They grumble about how many times can they call and say 'I'm following up.'"*

Without following up, however, the technicians can kiss those potential clients goodbye. According to Marketing Donut, 80 percent of sales leads require five follow-ups after the initial contact to get the sale. Yet, only 8 percent of salespeople follow up five times.

I get it. Without having a system, concrete ideas, or a motive other than "I'm following up," we get stuck. I've been there.

When working with my clients, we develop an intentional list of concrete ideas with an email campaign that plays off the yearly seasons.

This jam-packed mini-book provides ideas, examples, and strategies so that you will always have an opportunity to reach out to potential clients. You'll find several QR Codes so that you can see examples that I have created, including articles, press releases, infographics and more.

You can't get sales if you can't re-engage your prospects.

Each strategy offers examples with a Make-It-Happen Action for you to take in a step-by-step format.

You can text, email, private message, or make calls using these strategies. Adjust your communication method to the one that your prospect prefers.

It's time to skip the useless "I'm checking in" messages! Instead, get more clients with intentional follow-up strategies.

Here's to re-engaging, reconnecting, and getting more clients! **Here's to Bouncing-Up Your Sales!**

Mj Callaway,
President, Mj Callaway Training & Development
Creator, Bounce-Up Principle

Strategy 1
Jog Their Memory With Three Bullets

One of my clients would send a "thank you" email to potential buyers. Yes, it's a great idea when talking with the buyer because you're showing gratitude for the time you spent together. However, a "thank you" after a connect kind of infers closure of a conversation, and in written format doesn't spark any subsequent dialogue.

A couple of weeks later, when my client wanted to reach out, she didn't know what to say and didn't have detailed notes of the conversation.

With this in mind, we created the three-bullet follow-up summary.

After thanking your future buyer, include something personal you learned about them. It could be about their family, a pet, a favorite professional team, or vacation. Or what professional tidbit did the prospect share? For example, did they receive a promotion or complete a certification? The goal is to reconnect to the recent conversation and build a stronger relationship.

The next step is the three-point summary:

During our great conversation, here are three points we discussed.

- *Point 1 – The reason/struggle they have. What caused them to reach out to you? What emotion do they feel?*

- *Point 2 – What is the outcome they want from working with you. How happy they will be when the problem is solved.*

- *Point 3 – The solution you gave to solve their problem.*

Looking forward to connecting next week.

Have a Bounce-Up day! (Add a company-related ending that makes you different and links your brand.)

Mj

The three-bullet wrap-up lets you re-engage with the original points covered during your conversation. Also, it builds specifically in the direction of continuing the dialogue at a later date, instead of closing off the dialogue.

Make-It-Happen Action:

1. Reflect on your last prospect conversation.

2. Jot down several points that you covered in the conversation.

3. Note the struggles and outcomes that your potential client wanted. Think of it as the pain they're facing because of the problem or challenge and the feeling of paradise they'll get when you solve their problem.

4. Choose the best points for the follow-up email.

5. Write and send the Three-Bullet Wrap-Up.

Strategy 2
It's Party Time With A Milestone Celebration

A family-owned moving and storage company I had as a client celebrated 50 years in business. What a milestone and an opportunity to share the good news with current clients, prospective clients, and vendors. Helping them plan the celebration with a yummy buffet, adult drinks, and soda, we included several fantastic swag items for the guests. Along with a logo-branded bottle of wine, we added a 5" x 7" glossy card with the company's grassroots story with photos from the late 1960s of the founder and his first company-owned truck.

Another family-owned business celebrated its 60th anniversary for its entertainment complex. During a conversation with the group sales manager, he asked for suggestions about using this special occasion to stand out from other entertainment complexes. To kick off this incredible milestone, gather park photos from the 1960s and 1970s. Then, post those pictures on their social platforms and ask followers to post their photos, too. Next, contact local media announcing the celebration and photo request.

A vintage photo collage in an email or printed postcard would be a joyful way to engage with potential clients. Again, the collection would be extraordinary to see. Plus, the vintage photos would enable the company to strengthen its brand awareness and creditability—the know, like, and trust factor.

Make-It-Happen Action:

1. Now, you don't have to be in business for 50 years. Maybe you're celebrating five years. It's an opportunity to share the memories to connect and engage authentically.

2. In all cases, send out a press release. Contact the press.

3. Then, send the media feature to your inquiry and prospect list.

4. Another strategy is to contact your local Mayor's office about getting a City Proclamation. This strategy works well for anniversary dates of ten years and beyond. Usually, you can fill out an online form. Be aware you need to do it six weeks before the anniversary celebration. Think of how exciting it would be to share a City of (name your city) Proclamation.

Strategy 3
Get Innovative With National Days

National Days are an innovative way to produce one-of-a-kind follow-up messages. You have 365 days for spin-off ideas so that you can reach out to potential clients.

Some of the National Days I've used for follow-up campaigns include Irish Coffee, Fun at Work, Celebration of Life, Salesperson, World Tourism, Women's Small Business Month, Popcorn, and Nonprofit.

For example, if you're in the entertainment industry, on August 16th, National Roller Coaster Day would be a fun way to promote your coasters with a photo or two for the visual. For anyone in the safety industry, March 4th is National Safety Day.

Imagine the endless possibilities. Once you have pinpointed a campaign (a specific National Day with content and photos), you're on your way to standing out from others in your industry. (You know, the competitors.)

Make-It-Happen Action:

1. Go to https://nationaldaycalendar.com/what-day-is-it/ and choose the day you want to use for your prospecting.

2. The current day works for immediate follow-up campaigns to a limited number of people.

3. For a campaign with numerous people, choose a future day for reaching out.

4. Create a fun graphic as a PNG or JPEG that you can insert into an email. By inserting the photo into your email, you decrease the

chance of your email going into a filter or spam folder.

5. Or make it a hard copy by designing a postcard that you can mail out.

Strategy 4
Do What Influencers Do

Visualize book or product reviewers and celebrity followers. They help promote products and people because they're raving fans. Reviewers and followers share their thoughts, experiences, and enjoyment. As a result, these raving fans attract non-customers and non-followers for authors, product creators, and celebrities.

That's what strategic testimonies can do for you.

"Dear Brandon-

First, are you staying warm during this crazy weather?

When I received this email from Sam, I thought of you. I remembered how much you liked Product A. You mentioned it would help your team streamline their workload. Here's how Sam said it helped his team."

Testimony (Skip a line and add the golden testimony in a noticeable font color to stand out.)

I'm curious if your team has similar challenges like Sam's team or something completely different? I'll give you a call Tuesday or Thursday this week.

Mj

Make-It-Happen Action:

1. Sort through your testimonies.

2. Segment them into different categories according to your customers: families, couples, retirees, and so forth. Or segment them into products or services.

3. Select the testimonies that evoke an emotion, share an experience or show a result. These testimonies make the most impact on potential buyers.

4. Create a personalized email. Include one testimony that shows how it will help/benefit/add value for the future client.

Bonus Action: Refer to the *Jog Their Memory With Three Bullets Strategy* from earlier in this book. You will always have a point to add to any follow-up actions you take.

Strategy 5
I Want What She's Having

You've all heard that a picture is worth a thousand words. However, a smiling face in that picture is worth double. Countless studies have shown that seeing a smile triggers an automatic muscular response and whether we know the other person or not, we smile, too. Plus, a smile lifts our mood, according to brain science.

What could be better than sending an email, a text, or a postcard with a photo of a smiling customer to potential buyers? So, let's spread those smiles to those we want to help solve their problems.

Make-It-Happen Action:
1. Capture a candid picture of a client smiling while using your product or service.

2. Get permission to use the photo.

3. Then, use an application (app) on your phone or laptop such as Canva, Phonto, or Font Candy to add a quote, phrase, or greeting to it.

4. Insert the JPEG into the body of the email or text. By inserting it into the body of the email, you have less chance of it going to a filter or spam folder.

5. Take it a step further and have a postcard designed from the photo.

Strategy 6
Invite To A Special Event

One of my clients, a regional custom home builder, struggled to get a face-to-face meeting using telephone and email inquiries. To create a non-committal invite, we combined a promotional offer with a home show booth invitation. The Home Show invite wouldn't be as big a commitment for the inquiry person as a visit to their showroom.

Here's an example of the email (names and locations changed for privacy).

Dear Brandon:

Get out of the cold! (Change this to reflect the season.)

We'll give you a warm welcome when you visit our ABC Custom Homes Booth #1999 at the Home and Garden Show from March 6th – 15th.

It's the largest Home Event in Pittsburgh. And we'll give you a certificate for $2500 in ABC Homes Design Selections for stopping by and saying hi.

And here's a tip for you. Buy your ticket online, and you'll receive a free one-year subscription to Better Homes and Garden Magazine, Fitness Magazine, or Every Day with Rachel Ray Magazine.

Here's the link:
www.HomeandGardenShow.visit

Mark your calendars, and we'll see you soon.

Remember, at ABC Homes, we treat you like part of our family!

Mj Callaway

P.S. If you would rather have a custom appointment, call me today at 000-000-0000.

Make-It-Happen Action:

1. What event would be a good one for your inquiry list? For example, do you set up as a vendor at trade shows? Do you have an open house that could work?

2. If not, what is a simple event to organize to invite your inquiry list? For example, could you partner with another business to share the workload and expense?

3. Once you have the details, follow this email format to invite your future buyers.

Strategy 7

Questions Are The Key To Unlocking Secrets

When working with one of my clients, a developer, we created a monthly email marketing campaign that went beyond the common sales-y approach. We wanted to get our prospects, those who had called, emailed, or visited a showroom, to think about what they wanted in their homes. Also, we showed we cared about their lifestyles when building their forever home. Our purpose was to create a stronger connection and relationship with them.

The list of questions hit the different types of customers my client would have.

Hi Brandon!

It's Mj here.

The end of May kicks off the picnic season. So when you're in your new ABC home, will you be the one to host picnics and parties?

It's a great question because you'll want to think about how you'll use your outdoor space when you're looking for land. Many times, homeowners-to-be might not think about all the ways they will use their outdoor spaces.

Here are six quick questions to consider:

- *Will you hold picnics and parties for family and friends?*

- *Will you need space to build play structures like a swing set or horseshoe pit?*

- *Are you one to enjoy morning coffee on a deck, patio, or pergola?*

- *Will you want an outdoor kitchen?*

- *Do you plan to have a vegetable garden?*

These questions will help you when you're looking for different lot sizes.

Enjoy,

Mj

P.S. How would you use your outdoor space? I would love to hear your ideas, especially ones I hadn't mentioned. Hit the reply. ☺

Make-It-Happen Action:

1. Start with one topic about your product, service, or company.

2. Identify what past clients have wanted and purchased. Keep in mind what someone wants versus what someone buys could be entirely different.

3. Construct a list of three to five questions. Keep it short so that the person will read it. Use bullets for easy reading.

4. Write the email following this format or a similar one.

5. Repeat the action with other topics.

> *If we're not getting the answers we want, we're not asking the right questions.* – Mjism

Strategy 8
Are You Making Life Easier For Buyers?

What tips do you know about your industry, product, or service? For example, a photographer can tell you what to wear and what not to wear to look more attractive on camera. A wedding planner can tell you the common money mistakes couples make when planning their wedding. An auto mechanic can share several reasons why your tires wear out faster than they should. My friend Cathy Droz, an expert in the auto industry, can rattle off ten mistakes car salespeople and dealerships make when selling to women.

Every professional has numerous tips of value that they can share. Make your tips the center of an email. Or turn them into a tips sheet or an infographic to share with your prospects.

Remember, the fundamental purpose is offering value.

Tips, tip sheets, and infographics provide an effective way to re-engage with prospects, start a conversation with a cold contact, and offer value to current clients.

Make-It-Happen Action:

1. Start writing down tips that you know. Then, highlight the ones that give the most value.

2. Three to seven tips work best. However, I like odd numbers such as five and seven.

3. Sort through your tips. Highlight the two most impactful ones. These would be your first and last tips. Start strong and end strong.

4. For your other tips, put them in a logical order.

5. Now, you can create a graphic with Canva or another program. Or have a graphic designer design it for you. You can always reach out on social media to find a graphic design student.

Strategy 9

Do You Have Ways To Save Buyers Time Or Money?

"How do I get my technicians to follow up after they've given a prospect an estimate?" asked the sales director of sizeable commercial heating and cooling company.

"They call the person once, maybe twice, then stop because they don't know what else to say besides have you made a decision or checking in."

This scenario has been said by sales managers and business owners many times. Tap into two things that concern most people, especially business executives—time and money. Think about all the consumer magazines. You'll see many magazine covers feature leads (what's on the front cover) boosting *Ways to Save Time/Money* and *Mistakes to Avoid.*

Here are two ideas to contemplate.

Idea A

Let's say the potential client is a manufacturing company. The last situation management wants to happen is to have the HVAC go down. Consider the amount of lost productivity if staff can't work due to extreme heat or lack of heat.

What will the manufacturing company lose in productivity, time, and money in this scenario? What's at risk? How many work hours are lost? If they can't fill orders, will they lose revenue?

Idea B

Another consideration is how much money the company will save by updating its heating and cooling units. The larger the square footage of a building, the greater the savings. With a few math calculations, the technicians could figure this out, which would benefit the client to know.

"Hello, Brandon!

I was thinking about your company and was curious how you could save with a new unit. So I did a few calculations with your square footage. When you do upgrade your air conditioner, you could save $XXXX a year."

Wow! I didn't realize it, did you?

Make-It-Happen Action:

1. Brainstorm how you, your product, service, or company can save your buyers time or money.

2. Think back to your customer conversations and what you have shared in the past.

3. Have customers gleaned savings along the way that you can share with others?

4. Next, construct a follow-up email template around these savings so that all you need to do is tweak it to send to your future clients.

5. Note: Personalize each email to send it out individually. You have less chance of it going to spam.

Strategy 10
Share A Valuable Article

How many articles do you come across in a week? From digital to printed format, probably, more than you realize.

The next time you're scanning through a magazine, digital newsletter, or blog, keep an eye out for content that could add value to your clients and prospects. For a printed article, snap a photo and email it. Or make a copy and mail it. Although we've gotten away from the latter, doing so gives you a leg up because you're making an effort and taking the time to copy and mail it. For digital content, copy the link and email or text it to your clients and prospects. Either way, sharing an article is a way to stay in touch with your audience.

Add a quick message. Here are a few ideas.

- *"When I read this article, I thought you would like it."*

- *"When I came across this article, it reminded me of our last conversation. Enjoy."*

- *"This article gave me a few ideas and thought it could give you some, too."*

Make-It-Happen Action:

1. What kind of articles and content would be of value to your prospects?

2. There could be different topics to fit your various clients and buyers.

3. Make a list of five topics that would be a good fit.

4. Find three articles that would work best for your audience.

5. Start a resource folder as you add more articles.

Strategy 11
Highlight A Startling Statistic

Midway through the global pandemic, I came across an alarming statistic around customer loyalty reported by McKinsey & Co.

Only 12 percent of consumers are continuing to stay with the same retailers/business.

After reading that statistic, what struck me was that out of 100 consumers, 88 of them planned to spend their money somewhere else. They were looking for new businesses, which meant opportunities for my clients and me.

I created an infographic referencing the McKinsey & Co. statistic with my branding and contact information.

How did I use it? First, I shared this infographic with all my past and current clients and sent it to prospects. Then, I shared it on my social platforms.

Make-It-Happen Action:

1. Look for a statistic that would make a powerful impression on your target market. You can search on Google for a specific statistic in your industry or market. Be sure to use a credible source.

2. Email or text the written statistic to your list.

3. Or take it a step further. Create an infographic using this statistic to reinforce your point of view. For example, flipping the statistic to sharing that it means 88 out of 100 consumers are looking for new businesses.

4. Include your branding and contact information.

5. Insert the graphic as a JPEG or PNG into the body of your email.

6. Send it out to your prospect list and clients who would find value in it.

Strategy 12

Promote An Icon Idea

How can you have fun with what you do or sell?

One of my program participants is the sales director for a multi-entertainment complex. Let's call him Brandon. The complex offers something for everyone. Sometimes, when there is so much to promote, it's hard to pinpoint what you promote. For example, the sales director has wanted to start a newsletter yet needed ideas on what to include.

Our brainstorming reminded me of the media trips I took as a travel writer a decade ago. The trips included several specific tracks, from food to golf to family. Once, there was even a beer track—yes, those writers tasted beer all week long.

Spinning off this idea, Brandon could create different icons or avatars—a specific type of person connected to a particular type of recreation.

With the multiple entertainment centers in mind, he could turn unique restaurants and food kiosks into Foodie Fun. Then, one month Brandon could cover Foodies in his newsletter. Additionally, he could design a one-sheet marketing piece dedicated to a Foodie Fun map. It's a distinctive way to reach out to prospects and past clients while making his entertainment complex stand out from the crowd.

Another month, Brandon could concentrate on Thrill Seekers and map out the quickest way to maneuver these popular rides in the complex. Other ideas include the Selfie Spotlight for the best spots for selfies and 'Tween/Teen Track for favorite 'tween and teen hangouts.

Make-It-Happen Action:

1. Choose one particular type of client according to your target audience.

2. What would be a creative category title for these buyers?

3. Brainstorm the details for the different icons that would coordinate with this category of buyers.

4. Write an email with these details for this first category. Or design a tip sheet, infographic, postcard, or graphic.

5. Once you have one avatar completed, you will become more efficient in inventing others.

Strategy 13
Be Our Podcast Guest

Podcast guest interviews can provide a profitable way to follow up while proving creditability. Think of your guest spot as a two-for-one. You get to share your insights about what you do and who you serve, as well as you get to talk about your product, service, or business.

Here are six compelling reasons why being a podcast guest makes sense.

Reason 1

Hosts will promote your episode and will ask you to promote it as well. This technique gives you an opportunity to re-engage with your prospects and current clients by sharing the upcoming details.

Reason 2

Once the episode has gone live, you'll get a replay link that you can share. Send a short email to your contact list saying, *"in case you missed it,"* here's the link to hear the replay.

Reason 3

Here's the exciting part that makes this technique even more valuable. In a survey of 300,000 podcast listeners, 63 percent of people bought something a host promoted, and 71 percent of those listeners said they visited the sponsor's website.

Reason 4

Most podcasters will ask you for your contact information and encourage you to talk about your product, service, or business.

Reason 5

You can include the episode link on your website and connect it to your YouTube channel.

Reason 6

You have something of value and excitement to share on your social media platforms.

Make-It-Happen Action:

1. Check out these two podcast sites that match hosts and guests: Matchmaker.fm and Podcastguests.com

2. Prep first. Decide what topic you can share with the podcaster's audience. Remember to add value in the interview.

3. Have your topics and a short bio ready to include when asked.

4. Write a list of three to five questions the host could ask. Consider the podcast audience when responding. Always add value.

5. Contact podcasters.

6. Take it away from here!

> *"Stand out! Be mint chocolate chip in a vanilla world."* - Mjism

And That's a Wrap!

13 Simple Client Follow-Up Strategies gives you the foundation to create engaging messages so that you can reconnect with potential clients who have ghosted you.

Use this mini-book to kick off your brainstorming to develop additional messages so that you never have to resort to those USELESS and BORING "I'm checking in" or "I'm following up" messages again.

Do you have an idea or a message you want to share? Or do you have a success story you want to share? Email me at Mj@MjCallaway.com. I'd love to hear from you.

And possibly, you could be my next guest on the *Bounce-Up™ Broadcast*!

Here's to creating messages that get more clients!

Here's to Bouncing-Up Your Sales!

Mj Callaway, CSP, CVP

Creator, *13 Simple Client Follow-Up Strategies Series*

Founder, *The Bounce-Up™ Principle*

ACKNOWLEDGEMENTS

- A heartfelt thank you to my kids, Deanna, Josh, and Kristy for being who you are and all you do. Love you and the g-kiddies with all my heart.

- A big thank you to my long-time friend Beverly Carrol for our deep conversations about life, love, business, goals and so much more. The hours fly by when we get on the phone.

- Thank you to my Quad City Mastermind, Lisa Ryan, Debbie Peterson, Maureen Zappala, and Annie Meehan for your business savvy and encouragement. You rock!

- Thank you to my seven-year accountability partner, Laura Greco who keeps me on track, brainstorms ideas and lends an ear.

- Another thank you goes out to Maria Brady, Elisabeth Connolly, Gail Gloeckl, Bob Pacanovsky and Josh Rulnick for support and amazing book endorsements.

- To my New York gals, Georgianna Koulianos and Kelly Salonica Staikopoulos, for sharing the book and business journey with me.

- Thank you to my clients and book launch team! You rock!

GET ADDITIONAL BOOKS

You can share this book with your corporation, organization, association, or team. Do you have a conference or annual meeting? Give a copy of *13 Simple Client Follow-Up Strategies* to your attendees. It makes a great addition to the swag bag, and it beats adding to your attendees' collection of water bottles from other events. You'll stand out!

We can customize this book by adding your logo and inserting a message from your President, CEO, or Chair with a minimum quantity of only 100.

We can offer a bulk price for book orders of 100 or more.

Contact Mj for more details:
Mj@MjCallaway.com

SPEAKER ~ AUTHOR ~ TRAINER ~ 2X SURVIVOR

About Mj Callaway, CSP, CVP

Mj Callaway delivers outcome-focused programs that include humor, real-world stories, and strategic self-mastery tools you can implement immediately. As a two-time cancer warrior and domestic abuse survivor, Mj shares that every setback is an opportunity to create your Bounce-Up™. You'll find Mj on stage with her sidekick Henry, an inflatable punching bag, and sometimes a basketball, beach ball, and bubbles. Audience members find Mj's energy and positive mindset contagious. As a speaker, trainer, and consultant, she speaks from 20 plus years in events management, marketing, sales, and publishing industries.

Mj's sales experience includes selling three times her annual sales quota as a top-five producer in a male-dominated industry. She's a certified sales professional, certified virtual presenter, and past president of the National Speakers Association, Pittsburgh. Her newly released book, *Bounce-Up: Outpower Adversity, Boost Resilience, Rebound Higher*, has been endorsed by the CEO of the Healthy Workforce Institute.

Fun facts about Mj:

- Sold a children's game to Disney

- Won four Gold Awards from Parenting Media Association

- Ziplined over gators in AL, biked down a volcano in HI, and played tug-of-war with a baby black bear in MI.

Mj Callaway's Programs and Books

Mj's Most Popular Remote and In-Person Keynotes and Programs:
https://www.mjcallaway.com/speaking

- Fearless Comebacks: Make Your Bounce Back Your Bounce-Up™

- Rev-Up Your Revenue: Build Your Resilient Driven Sales Plan

- Power Team: Grow Your Business/Sales with Your Circle of Influence

- Rock Your Sales Trivia with Training

Check Out Mj's Digital Programs:
https://www.mjcallaway.com/courses

- Selling in a COVID World

- Power Team: Grow Your Business with Your Circle of Influence

See Mj's Books:
https://www.mjcallaway.com/books-c

- *Bounce-Up: Outpower Adversity, Boost Resilience, REBOUND Higher*

- *Sales Success Roadmap: Your GPS to Boost Your Sales*

- *13 Simple Client Follow-Up Strategies: Skip Useless "Checking In" Messages and Get More Sales*

- *Twenty WON: 21 Female Entrepreneurs Share Their Stories of Business Resilience During a Global Pandemic*

GET FREE RESOURCES TO GENERATE RESULTS!

Grab Your Free Toolkits:

- Grab Your FREE Sales Toolkit: https://www.mjcallaway.com/bounce-up-sales-toolkit

- Grab Your FREE Resilient Workplace Toolkit: https://www.mjcallaway.com/resilient-workplace-toolkit

Get More Free Resources Here:

- https://www.mjcallaway.com/free-downloads

Get Free Weekly Bounce-Up™ Tips:

- https://www.mjcallaway.com/bounceup chronicles

KEEP IN TOUCH WITH MJ CALLAWAY

Contact Mj Callaway:

Email: Mj@MjCallaway.com

Site: www.MjCallaway.com

Connect with Mj Callaway on Social Media:

https://www.facebook.com/BounceUpCommunity (for entrepreneurs & businesses)

https://www.linkedin.com/in/mjcallaway/

https://twitter.com/MjCallawaySpeak

https://www.youtube.com/c/MjCallaway

https://www.instagram.com/mjcallawayspeaker/

WHAT SOME SPEAKING & TRAINING CLIENTS SAY...

"I don't know how you do it. Our employees groan because they don't want to participate in the training. Then, they walk out of the first session smiling." – Bill M., Human Resources Director

"Mj delivered a high energy and engaging lunch and learn for my team. She provided techniques and stories that got everyone thinking on how to approach and respond to change from a positive perspective. I highly recommend her as a speaker/motivator." – Jackie L., COO

"I continue to have the privilege to hire Mj Callaway as a webinar presenter for my company, PCI Webinars. She is an engaging expert with top-notch content and delivery. I've also had the honor of co-presenting a webinar with her that was not only fun,

but it was also a huge success for my nationwide clients. If you are looking for an online presenter with passion and bounce that not only engages and educates her audiences, but also inspires them to be their best, Mj Callaway will likely be a great fit for your organization and next event." – Andrew Sanderbeck, Managing Partner, PCI

"Mj, I really enjoyed your Power Team presentation. I filled out the ABA survey and I listed you as the best speaker." – Karl P., CDME, CASE

"I absolutely love how vibrant and calm you are at the same time. I love the way you explain and break things down. I would recommend your session to any of my peers"! - Chevonne Torrence, Tourism Sales Manager, Tuscaloosa Tourism and Sports

"Mj, I found your personality and presentation delightful! You reinforced and inspired me to think outside the box. I'm adding and suggesting experiences, instead of just the regular live music

shows that people expect to see in Branson, MO." – Patty Nilges, Group Sales Director, Branson

*"I can't rave enough about Mj Callaway's **sales training**. With each thought-provoking session, we **dug deeper into sales strategy** and designed a road map specifically for selling my product. By the end of my 8-session program, we had created an **easy-to-follow company sales manual** to use to train my salespeople as they come on board. When I started with Mj, I was a businesswoman who loved my work but hated selling my product. She taught me to **think differently about my definition of selling**. I never thought I could be this excited about sales."* - Kiya Tomlin, Kiya Tomlin

TESTIMONIES FOR *13 SIMPLE CLIENT FOLLOW-UP STRATEGIES*

"Mj Callaway's proven tips for creatively connecting resonates throughout this helpful book! Apply just a few tips and watch your profitability increase." Maria T. Bernardo Brady, President Marakae Marketing, Inc., Curator of I Chose Happy.Live and Best-Selling Author

"Mj Callaway makes it easy for you to do the little things for your business to help it grow! The "Make-it-Happen Action" in each of her chapters gives you the step-by-step way on how to outsmart your competition. You don't need to reinvent the wheel when it comes to doing those things that will keep you top of mind with your customers, Mj has already done it for you!" – Bob Pacanovsky, Chief Hospitality Officer, Keynote Speaker at The Black Tie Experience

"Even in the professional services sector, we can sometimes struggle with the follow up to client proposals and staying connected with existing clients. I love Mj Callaway's ideas for connecting with your prospective clients with Strategy #10, Sharing a Valuable Article. I think this would really speak to prospects and existing clients alike to let them know that you had them top of mind. As a CPA serving small to medium-sized businesses and their owners, I would expect that Strategy #13 would be a great way to showcase my ideas on saving money on taxes and making your financial life more organized. I love Mj's energy and approach to ditching the ho-hum follow-ups and inserting your own brand of connection." - Elizabeth S. Connolly, CPA, President, Author, Connector Connolly Steele + Company

"Mj Callaway delivers creative and practical follow-up strategies in a conversational style. Mj takes out the mystery of what to say in your follow-

up message. Mj simplifies your follow-up system with actionable steps, email templates, and fun examples. This book is a must-have for anyone in business." – Josh Rulnick, Founder, Zire Nutrition LLC Director of Business, R&R Express, Inc.

My Next Steps:

Made in the USA
Middletown, DE
13 April 2022